"If you want to get 'unstuck' in your walk with Christ, work through this book and put its principles into practice. Nate Akin takes us back to the basics; back to our 'first love'. His core truths offer the help you need to rekindle the passion that propels you forward in Christlikeness. These are not mere facts to know but life altering truths to live."

Donna Gaines, Founder & President of ... E2Read.org

"Nate Akin delivers ... liever
needs: a go...
the fou...
somethi... t
was neve...

Betsy Góm... a

"If you are lik... e, you sometimes get spiritually stuck. Stuck in reading your Bible, praying, and just following Jesus on mission in the world. Nate Akin has written the perfect antidote for us! This brief but blessed book will bolster your walk with God and put new wind in your spiritual sails."

James Merritt, Senior Pastor of Cross Pointe Church, Duluth, Georgia and former President of the Southern Baptist Convention

~~Static~~

~~Stalled~~

Stuck?

Recapturing your joy in Christ

~~Static~~
~~Stalled~~
Stuck?

Recapturing your joy in Christ

Nate Akin

10 Publishing
a division of 10 of those.com

To my beloved children, Ada and Ryland:
I pray daily that you will find unceasing joy in
"Jesus Christ the faithful witness, the firstborn
of the dead, and the ruler of kings on earth.
To him who loves us and has freed us from
our sins by his blood" (Rev. 1:5).

First published in Great Britain in 2025

British Library Cataloguing in Publication Data
A record for this book is available from the British Library

ISBN: 978-1-83728-060-5

Designed by Tiger Finch Creatives

Printed in the UK

10Publishing, a division of 10ofthose.com
6b Upper Water Street, Newry, Co Down, Northern Ireland, BT34 1DJ

info@10ofthose.com
www.10ofthose.com

1 3 5 7 10 8 6 4 2

Contents

Introduction: Back to Basics

Have you ever been stuck? Stuck in a car ride you don't want to be in? Stuck in a meeting while fighting to keep your eyes open? Maybe worse, have you ever been stuck in a crawlspace or other small, enclosed place?

In one hilarious scene from the sitcom *The Office*, Pam plays a prank on Dwight in which she gets a co-worker to switch the wiring on the elevator's "circus board" so that when Dwight presses certain buttons, the elevator does the exact opposite. The prank works at first as Dwight exclaims, "The elevator is disobeying us!" Soon, however, the prank backfires and the elevator loses power all together. Pam is trapped with Dwight as he cries, "We are stuck! We are stuck!"

In a much more serious way, have you ever been stuck in an area of your life that matters most? Have you ever been stuck in your relationship with the Creator of your mind, body, and soul?

Being stuck is always challenging. But when you are spiritually stuck, struggling in your relationship with your Creator and Savior, it can be incredibly painful as well as hard to know how to move on from that place. I can empathize.

I grew up in a Christian home, coming to faith aged nine, and I now serve in Christian ministry. Yet I have experienced being stuck in my relationship with Christ many times. They have been seasons where I've felt trapped in by my sin, with no power to break out. I still remember one particularly hard but formative season full of sin, pain, repentance, and confession, where I felt like a spiritual leper, not knowing where to turn.

In other seasons my heart has been at times cold, dull, or weighed down. There have been times when living the Christian life did not seem as "fun" as living a non-Christian life, and the disciplines that are supposed to characterize us seemed dutiful rather than delightful. There have been times when I've driven to a Sunday service full of apathy; joylessly trying to work up the willpower to attend—or worse lead—the worship service.

Perhaps for you, church attendance is becoming less frequent, reading the Bible feels lifeless, and prayer feels like a slog. Or maybe life has become so busy that Jesus is all but squeezed out. The thought of sitting down and praying sounds great, but right now the kids need a ride, dinner needs making, and work has spilled into the evening. Christian discipleship has been swallowed up in surviving this stage of life.

—

In John Bunyan's classic book *The Pilgrim's Progress*, two friends, Christian and Hopeful, speak about a man they know called Turn-back. Together they chart the process of someone falling away from the faith. It begins in the mind and heart: Turn-back and his friends "draw off their thoughts all that they may from the remembrance of God, Death, and Judgment to come." This then affects their private actions such as prayer and curbing sin. Next they begin to "shun the company of lively and warm

Christians" and neglect church. As their friends change, hearts harden and sin is played with more openly until "being launched again into the gulf of misery, unless a Miracle of Grace prevent it, they everlastingly perish in their own deceivings."[1]

As you pick up this book, I don't know where you are in your spiritual pilgrimage. I don't know where you are in your relationship with Christ. Maybe you're caught in a momentary rut and need a refresher in your discipleship. Perhaps you're feeling desperate as I have in the past, knowing truth in your head but unable to see the light of Christ with your heart. Or maybe, like the character that Bunyan describes in *The Pilgrim's Progress*, you are backsliding in your faith. Being completely honest with yourself, you know if you don't do something now, you might not be in church in a year's time or still calling yourself a Christian in a decade.

Bunyan wrote his words to warn those in danger of giving up. And like this book, the warning is a call—not to despair, but an encouragement to be dissatisfied with stagnating and instead fan the flames of your love for Christ.

As I've come through my own times of spiritual slump, God has graciously given me a clearer understanding of how to possess and pursue joy in my relationship with the Lord. My aim in this book is to share some of this experience with you. Whatever your situation, my prayer is that this book will help you move from feeling stuck to flourishing in the faith once again.

–

It's become part of American football folklore that at the start of each new season the Green Bay Packers Hall of Fame coach, Vince Lombardi, would gather his players around him, hold up the oval ball, and say, "Gentlemen, *this* is a football." He was making the point that if they were going to succeed that season, then they would have to start back with the fundamentals.

In our own spiritual lives, whether we are progressing, stagnating, or going backward, the basics are always the place to go to. One of the wonderful things about Scripture is that it shows us how believers across the ages have done this.

Luke, the author of Acts, tells us that the first church were people with "glad and generous hearts" (Acts 2:46). Doesn't that sound great? So, how did they get to that place of joy? Luke describes it in this way:

> "So those who received his word were baptized, and there were added that day about three thousand souls. And they devoted themselves to the apostles' teaching and the fellowship, to the breaking of bread and the prayers. And awe came upon every soul, and many wonders and signs were being done through the apostles. And all who believed were together and had all things in common. And they were selling their possessions and belongings and distributing the proceeds to all, as any had need. And day by day, attending the temple together and breaking bread in their homes, they received their food with glad and generous hearts, praising God and having favor with all the people. And the Lord added to their number day by day those who were being saved." (Acts 2:41–47)

These seven verses provide the remedy we need. In the coming chapters I want to unpack Luke's cure in more detail but, for now, let me quickly highlight five things.

1. Those first believers "received his word," meaning Peter's gospel proclamation. In other words, they were saved and shaped by the *gospel*.
2. They were devoted to the apostles' teaching of the *Scriptures*.
3. They were committed to *prayer*.
4. They were dedicated "to the fellowship," that is, to the *church*.
5. They prioritized *mission* as they shared their faith with others. As Luke makes clear, the church grew as the Lord added to their number.

Gospel. Scriptures. Prayer. Church. Mission.

Each is a gift of grace from your Heavenly Father who wants to return you to a place of joy in him, even in the hardest of circumstances (see Hab. 3:17–19). Dear reader, let me encourage you, if you are feeling stuck or stagnant, to return to the basics as a way to fuel your soul in the same way.

1

The Gospel

So those who received his word were baptized …

As I think back to some of the times I was stuck, my experience was certainly clouded by sin that led to hurt. Those twin giants left me feeling unloved and unlovable, by people and by God. Could I have told you what the gospel was at those times? Probably. But it was having very little impact on the state of my heart. I was stuck. The issue was that I had not yet learned how to apply the gospel to my life for becoming more Christlike.

Growing up, I had somehow confusedly thought that being a Christian meant believing the gospel and then moving on to live a moral life. I missed that being a Christian meant leaning on and learning and loving the gospel for a lifetime rather than it just being the gateway in. It took me a long time to understand that the gospel is both the way in to the Christian faith and the way on in the faith. Over time I learned that the gospel is also the way out of being stuck.

As we go back to basics, we need to get clear in our minds what makes us a Christian. Really understanding the gospel is the first step to letting it transform your Christian life. Then, crucially, we need to fight to *really believe* the gospel not just with our minds but deep in our souls for our sanctification, or growth, in Christ.

So let's remind ourselves: What is the gospel message? At heart, it is a message of substitution.

In the Garden of Eden, humanity's parents willfully rebelled against their Creator and his Word. They were told by Satan that if their disobeyed God then they would become like God. Tragically, all of Adam and Eve's descendants (that's everyone, by the way) willfully walk in sin, too. In other words, Adam and Eve's sin plunged the whole world into a curse and three things (at least) were devastatingly broken as a result.

First, humanity's relationship with God: in the beginning Adam and Eve communed with God; after the Fall they hid from him.

Second, humanity's relationships with one another were broken: in Genesis 3 God makes it clear that from now on, Eve's "desire shall be contrary to your husband" (Gen. 3:16). The brokenness of human relationships descends so quickly that it's only a chapter later that Cain murders his own brother. Third, the creation itself is broken: as God makes clear, "cursed is the ground because of you" (Gen. 3:17).

This sin and brokenness invades our whole existence. No wonder work is hard and unsatisfying and relationships feel strained or distant. No wonder we struggle with our ego or lack of self-worth. Disappointment and hurt are ever present. Our hearts naturally veer us away from God and not toward him.

When feeling stuck, it's easy to fall into the trap of putting hope in a change of circumstances, thinking: "It'll be easier when ..." But the gospel tells us: It won't! Life will always throw us a challenge. Sin will always be there. This is one of the reasons you can't put off sorting out spiritual stagnation until you move out of home, or get a job, or the kids grow up, or you retire. If we just allow ourselves to drift for the time being, our hearts will naturally grow colder, not more spiritually alive. We need to act, but thankfully we're not left to sort it out on our own.

Despite the damage caused by Adam and Eve's sin, in the very chapter describing their punishment, God makes a promise that one day he would send someone who would defeat Satan and fix what was broken (Gen. 3:15). Centuries later, a man from Nazareth comes along who lived, died, and rose again to reverse the curse—restoring humanity's relationship with God, drawing his people together, and showing he has power over the brokenness of creation.

How is it that Jesus undoes the curse of Genesis 3? By substitution. As the apostle Paul writes, "Christ redeemed us from the curse of the law by becoming a curse for us" (Gal. 3:13). In other words, Jesus deals with the curse by taking the thorns that come out of the ground on his head at the cross. Jesus provides a way for us to be made right with God; he deals with our sin and the final penalty of that sin—death—by coming back to life. Jesus did all that was necessary for our forgiveness, salvation, adoption, and future glory.

If you have never believed this gospel message then you are not stuck, but lost. Today is the day to repent and turn from your sin, and put your faith in Christ alone. Know this: Jesus freely welcomes you. In Acts 2:41–47 Luke tells us that Christians are those who have believed the message of the gospel. Thousands turned from sin to God as Peter preached about Jesus' death and resurrection, and they immediately got baptized and formed the first church.

That is why the message is called the gospel—it is *good* news. Actually, it's more than that—it's the *best* news. If we are trusting Jesus, we will not face eternal judgment but are saved for a restored relationship with God. Moreover, he fills us with his Spirit to transform us.

Believe It (Head)

Perhaps the chapter so far has been familiar ground for you. You know all this. And you still feel totally stuck.

A good way out of a rut is to remind yourself again and again who you are in Christ and, therefore, how loved by God you really are. See yourself the same way God sees you. He sees you *in* Christ, which means that he views you in the same way he views his beloved Son. Please believe this. You are not merely tolerated by God. You are loved by God. Even in your sin or spiritual apathy.

Why not stop reading for a moment and jot down a few words that describe how God feels about Jesus?

Now look again at your list: this is how the Father feels about you.

When you struggle to be impacted by the truths you know, be like the dad who comes to Jesus in Mark 9. His son was possessed by an unclean spirit and, as he struggles to have faith that Jesus can heal him, he prays, "I believe; help my unbelief!" (Mark 9:24). This prayer is powerful when you are stuck, stagnant, or doubting.

Love It (Heart)

The Maker of heaven and earth has set his affections on you and demonstrated it in the most glorious and visible way possible. Even though you were a rebel, he loved you with a saving love and sent his Son to die on a cross for you.

It's not enough to just believe this when you're stuck; you need to embrace it.

When your heart falters in its love of the gospel, do what you can to find verses, hymns, lyrics, and quotes that will help stoke your passion again to remind you of what God has done for you in Christ. Sometimes a familiar truth expressed in a poetic or unusual way can cause us to appreciate it afresh. At other times it's not something new, but something precious that can get past our jadedness. I like to recall hymns I learned as a child to fan my happiness in the Lord.

And it's not just the words. Music itself is a gift which can rekindle our souls, so find a playlist for when you shave or shower or straighten your hair each morning and allow the songs to prepare your heart for the day while you prepare your body.

Act on It (Hands)

The gospel does not just save sinners; it sanctifies saints. When we have lost joy in our spiritual walk, the very thought of fighting sin may sound oppressive, but it's sin that makes us miserable, not holiness. Just ask Adam and Eve. Sin promises so much and delivers slavery. If we want to know true joy again, we need to apply the gospel to struggles with sin.

Growing up, my father used to give me and my brothers a very easy way to identify what is at the heart of our sin. He told us to consider the phrase, "I need Jesus + ___________." Whatever we fill that blank in with is an idol at the heart of our sin. And it does not matter if you fill it in with good things—health, a spouse, family, good job—or with sinful things—greed, lust, power. Just as Adam and Eve discovered, the idol will not deliver. Eventually it'll disappoint us or become a tyrant over us. It sucks out life and replaces it with death. And we get caught in its trap.

I love the quote from the nineteenth-century preacher Thomas Chalmers, who said:

> "There is not one of these transformations in which the heart is left without an object. Its desire for one particular object may be conquered; but as to its desire for having some one object or other, this is unconquerable ... The only way to dispossess the heart of an old affection is by the expulsive power of a new one."[2]

Just trying to "do better" is not the gospel way. It will not produce lasting and enduring joy either from our sin or our complacency. I guarantee that will result in feeling more stuck than ever. Instead, we must replace sin with even greater love for the Lord. We should dwell on Jesus, seeing his beauty, his patience, his compassion, his love. When I was at my lowest, I needed to know the truth of the gospel and feel the impact of God's love. This was my turning point in fighting sin. Jesus came to mean more to me than any idol.

—

As we move on in the next chapters to think about our need to hear from God, pray, commit to meeting with other Christians, and engage in mission, remember that we are in no way earning God's favor through any of this. We pursue these things because he has saved us, not in order to be saved. In your struggles with spiritual apathy and duty-driven service, in your prayerlessness and your irregular church attendance, the Father looks at you and says, "my beloved child." And just like the Father in the Parable of the Prodigal

Son, our Heavenly Father does not just walk to meet us with outstretched arms; he runs.

2

The Scriptures

And they devoted themselves to the apostles' teaching ...

Put yourself in the scene. Our Lord is in the final days before the cross. He's riding on a donkey through the middle of cheering crowds. Very likely some from those crowds will also be ones crying "crucify him" on Good Friday.

As he enters Jerusalem, Jesus knows that the time to die has come. As he teaches the crowd, he lets them in on his anguish: "Now is my soul troubled. And what shall I say? 'Father, save me from this hour'? But for this purpose I have come to this hour. Father, glorify your name!"

Immediately, something extraordinary happens. A voice comes from heaven: "I have glorified it, and I will glorify it again" (John 12:27–28). In that moment, the crowd audibly hears God speak.

I'm guessing that's never happened to you.

Or has it?

Mind-blowingly, when we read the Scriptures we hear the very voice of God (2 Pet. 1:20–21). God himself speaks to us. To you! And his words are powerful, life-giving, and joy-producing.

In Acts 2:42, the early church was devoted to the apostles' teaching as they explained from the Scriptures how Jesus fulfilled the promises and prophecies of the Old Testament. The apostles' teaching strengthened them, gave wisdom and direction, and most of all, pointed them to Christ. Their relationship with God flourished, as all relationships do, with communication. They knew if they wanted to enjoy and know God, they needed to hear from him.

Now I'm sure nearly everyone reading this book knows Christians should be listening to God regularly, but—honestly—when we're struggling spiritually, Bible reading often feels like a burden. Even if we are still opening up the pages each day, the words can at times seem dull and lifeless. When we go to church and Scripture is preached, the words can wash over us without connection. We've lost our taste for God's Word and chances are, it's having less and less impact on our lives. My guess is that if you're feeling spiritually stuck, the Bible no longer feels like it's God speaking to you.

It may be that you've allowed other things to gradually crowd God's voice out, or maybe God's clear teaching on an issue in the Bible feels uncomfortable and you're tempted to listen more to the world than to God. Either way, the Scriptures are no longer as alive as they once were to you and as they actually are.

Friends, there's a real danger of being deaf to the voice of God. The crowd in John 12 heard God answer his Son from heaven but could not understand what was happening and they surmised it must just be thunder, or maybe an angel (v. 29). God spoke and they missed it. It's tragically easy for us to do the same. So, how can we have—to borrow the words of Jesus—ears to hear?

Believe It (Head)

If we are going to get out of our rut, we must first believe that the Bible is truly the Word of God and that we need it. Consider this then by way of belief and the claim we make about the Bible: God wrote a book! Paul says the words were "breathed out by God" (2 Tim. 3:16). And you have access! Every Sunday together and every day on your own, you get to hear and read this book.

Of course, not every Christian is called into the ministry or to go to seminary, but every Christian is called to be a student of the Bible. We dig deep into God's Word not to primarily build up knowledge but to know God for ourselves. He reveals himself through his words and as he does so, the Spirit shapes us and transforms our minds and hearts, and our outlook on life and eternity.

Our worldview is going to be shaped by something. If the Bible is not our final authority, then ultimately we are like a man building his house upon the sand. Simply absorbing the beliefs of friends, family, and colleagues will not be enough when the storms of life hit. Culture and tradition prove to be shaky foundations for life. Relying on our experience or emotions will result in a pile of bricks when the waves splash in. Perhaps that's how you are feeling now. Only the words of Jesus provide the solid rock we need—we neglect them at great personal cost (Mt. 7:24–27).

Love It (Heart)

Second, for our renewal and joy we must love the Scriptures knowing that here we find the words of life. David tells us directly in Psalm 19:7 that they're "reviving [to] the soul." When we're feeling spiritually flat, it's so easy to crave distraction or entertainment—anything to feel that dopamine hit. Netflix and Instagram or even endless scrolling on social media are like candy to the soul, and we easily end up rejecting the nutrients of God's Word in favor of a sugar rush. But we need to retrain our taste buds, because spiritual health comes from a proper diet.

Just like trying to give up refined sugar, it's going to be hard, so we need to pray that the Holy Spirit would open our ears, eyes, and hearts to really *enjoy* God through his Word. I would encourage you to consider what passages in particular stir your affections to God. Try turning to a familiar passage that has struck you in the past and ask the Holy Spirit to strike you afresh through it.

If you don't know where to start, here are some ideas from the Psalms:

- Psalm 1 for when you need to refocus on God's Word.
- Psalm 23 for when you feel lost.
- Psalm 27 for when the world is pressing in.
- Psalm 42 for when you feel God is absent.
- Psalm 51 for when you are conscious of sin.
- Psalm 121 for when you feel attacked or afraid.

It is important to read all of the Scriptures but in dark moments, find portions that spark your heart and return to them again and again. If things are very dark, I urge you to ask a trusted friend to send you a short message or voice note each day, which includes a verse and brief prayer.

Act on It (Hands)

As we fight to retrain our taste buds, we might need to get creative. Scripture is designed to be heard as well as read. Could you listen to a Gospel as you drive to work, pleading with God to reveal himself through the Word as you turn the key in the engine each morning? Could you ask your roommate, spouse, or child to read a verse out loud over dinner each evening before saying grace? Could you listen to a sermon as you clean the bathroom or go for a run each week?

As well as being intentional about reading or listening to a portion of the Scriptures daily, why not pick a small passage to memorize? Again, don't make it some great undertaking (aim for a verse or two rather than the whole of Romans). Just do a little to hide God's Word in your heart.

We can often think very individually in the West, but knowing and enjoying God through his Word is a whole church activity. Go to services ready to be an active listener during the sermon. Having a notebook and pen works for some. Pray God would speak to you all. Seek to cultivate a disposition that is eager to hear the Word. And then gather with other believers to read and discuss it.

Even if you don't feel like it and would give anything to take a bath or scroll on your phone rather than head out on a weekday evening to Bible study, remind yourself that God speaks when his people gather around his Word. Go through your calendar now and put in a recurring entry for the church service and your mid-week group, making this your first commitment before the rest of the week fills up. Then why not give permission to a friend to keep you accountable to turning up each week?

–

When Jesus was tempted to look for provision elsewhere, he answered Satan, "It is written: 'Man shall not live on bread alone, but by every word that comes from the mouth of God'" (Mt. 4:4). God's Word is life to us, because there we find him. Remember, God's Word stands forever (Is. 40:8); is sharper than a two-edged sword (Heb. 4:12); is pure (Ps. 12:6) and true (Prov. 30:5). The Scriptures make us wise for salvation (2 Tim. 3:15); are a lamp to our feet (Ps. 119:105); and sanctify us (John 17:17). The true and lasting joy we seek won't come from anywhere else.

The Word of God is powerful—so powerful, it can change history in a way governments and militaries cannot. It can change the eternities of billions. When Martin Luther turned the world upside down in the Reformation, he attributed his success to the Bible:

> "I simply taught, preached, and wrote God's Word; otherwise I did nothing. And while I slept, or drank Wittenberg beer with my friends … the Word so greatly weakened the papacy that no prince or emperor ever inflicted such losses upon it. I did nothing; the Word did everything."[3]

If God's Word is that powerful, it can transform you.

3

The Prayers

... they devoted themselves to ... the prayers.

I still remember how I felt on 9/11 after hearing of the planes crashing into the Twin Towers. I was away from home and one of the things I remember most is that I just wanted to call my dad. I just thought, "If I can hear my dad's voice, then I will know everything is going to be okay." In an even greater way, prayer is a direct line of communication with our Heavenly Father.

Yet, even in times of spiritual growth, prayer often feels a struggle for me—in fact of all the ways to find joy, this is personally the hardest. Sometimes I sit down to pray and ten minutes later I realize I've been replaying a conversation I had yesterday or planning work or simply staring out the window. The more tired I am, the harder it becomes. The more stressed I am, the more artificial my words. The more battered by life's storms, the less energy I have to even try. The seasons when we know we most need to depend on God can be the times that prayer seems almost impossible.

So when it's just too hard on our own, we need to enlist Christian friends to pray for us and with us, knowing prayer is too important to neglect. But be encouraged: as we struggle, we can know there is always one friend who is praying for us—Jesus.

The writer to Hebrews tells us Jesus "is able to save to the uttermost those who draw near to God through him, since he always lives to make intercession for them" (Heb. 7:25). Jesus lives to pray for us, his people. For me. For you. You are never without an advocate before the Father.

This spurs us on to pray ourselves, and even when our words dry up or we are struggling, there's another person turning to the Father on our behalf. We read: "the Spirit helps us in our weakness. For we do not know what to pray for as we ought, but the Spirit himself intercedes for us with groanings too deep for words" (Rom. 8:26). When we are in a prayerless pit, we can simply cry out along with the Son and the Spirit, "Help, Lord!" and know it's a plea the Father loves to answer.

But, we don't want to stop there. If we want to have a flourishing faith, we need to desire to be people of prayer, like those in Acts 2. Prayer becomes a burden when we think it's just another demand upon our busy lives rather than our lifeline to our Father. We want to reach a place where we again believe in prayer's goodness and in its power. We want to love communing with God once more.

Believe It (Head)

If you could talk to anyone in the world, who would it be? Would you want to have a conversation with a political leader, an athlete, an actor perhaps? I played basketball in college, which means I would probably pick Michael Jordan. I'd love the chance to sit down over a meal and talk to him for as long as he would talk to me!

Friends, it's not just a famous person we can talk to. If we are in Christ, we have unhindered and unlimited access to the One who created everything—including Michael Jordan. What a privilege! We have the ear of God Almighty. And while I would love to speak about my hopes, dreams, concern, and worries with Michael Jordan (however unlikely!), it's not going to change my circumstances or the world. Talking to God will.

Could it be that sometimes, deep down, we don't really believe there is power in prayer?

It is widely attributed to the early-twentieth-century preacher, Samuel Chadwick, that he said:

> "The one concern the devil has is to keep Christians from praying. He fears nothing from prayerless studies, prayerless work, and prayerless religion. He laughs at our toil, mocks at our wisdom, but he trembles when we pray."

The devil trembles because God answers prayer, bringing down the kingdom of darkness and bringing in the Kingdom of God. It feels risky, but can I encourage you to pray specific prayers and see how God works in a situation. As you do, let me also encourage you to think about the immense privilege of prayer—it is a direct line of communication with the Creator God who has the power to transform hearts and lives.

Love It (Heart)

In God's kindness, I have been blessed with a wonderful mother. Her name is Charlotte and she raised four sons, which means (unfortunately for her) that she basically lived in a male dormitory for two decades of her life.

Throughout my upbringing (and beyond) she has proved herself to be a godly and loving woman. Yet, many people who know her don't realize that from the age of nine she grew up in a children's home because her parents were neglectful alcoholics. During those formative years of her life, her parents were largely absent. In fact, I recall her once being asked if she remembered the last time she saw her mother before moving out. I will never forget her reply. She said, "I remember sitting on the porch at our house and she came and slapped me off a bench, swore at me, and said she blamed me for being moved to the home." She didn't see her mother again until adulthood.

In the same way, she recalled how her dad often promised to visit on a weekend. My mother would get up early on those Saturdays, put on her nicest dress, and sit on the front porch of her cottage and wait. For hours. For a dad who never showed.

Friends, we must constantly remind ourselves that our Heavenly Father is not like that. We have an altogether different type of Father. We have a Father who cares for us, provides for us, who wants to hear from us, and who is always there for us. Do not forget it!

The theologian J.I. Packer even went as far to say that adoption "is the highest privilege that the gospel offers."[4] Again, just consider what is ours in the gospel: The Creator God has adopted us, he has chosen us, he has set his love upon us, and he has opened a line of communication to us in his Word and from us in prayer. This is the staggering reality for us: We have unhindered access to God and can approach him with confidence because of the blood of Jesus.

Act on It (Hands)

In light of the struggle to pray, I thought it would

be useful to list some practical applications to help in prayer.

1. Pray the Lord's Prayer. Do not pray for show or for your own glory; instead follow the pattern that Jesus taught us. First, pray for God's glory and then for your victory over sin, then for your own daily needs and the needs of others.
2. Pray the Bible. Study the prayers of the Bible such as Ephesians 3:14–21 and Philippians 1:9–11, and use them as the basis for your own prayers.
3. Set aside time to prayer. Like anything else, this takes discipline. But start small and build up.
4. Pray with other believers.
5. Ask a more mature Christian for help. I bet there are many Christians in your church who have struggled with prayer and would love to walk you through what has helped them. Hearing about the answers to prayer they've received can also spur you on.

6. Use a book of set prayers such as *The Valley of Vision*.
7. Remember that God hears you. The reformer Martin Luther famously made the point that we must not forget that God listens to our prayers. He said that we must remind ourselves we can know with complete certainty and absolute truth that God hears our prayers.

Perhaps above all, remember that our Lord Jesus vacated a tomb, ascended to our Father's side, and now lives forever to intercede for us. So, pray as though the divine audience awaits—because he does. Pray like a worshipper praising God; like a missionary hearing about the mission; like a soldier ready to take orders; like a subject talking to the King; like a beggar asking for bread; like the tax collector pleading for forgiveness; and like a child calling out to her father, knowing that when she does, he will not leave her waiting on the cottage porch.

4

The Church

… they devoted themselves to … the fellowship, to the breaking of bread.

As a young kid I remember being taught a hand gesture at our church. You probably know it. You interlock your hands and say, "Here's the church." Then you extend your index fingers to touch each other, "Here's the steeple," before opening your hand to reveal your fingers, "Open it up and see all the people." I can't quite remember the exact point in being taught it but one thing I do know: It's not consistent with the biblical idea of what a church is. In the New Testament, the church is not a building; it's not even an event. The church is a people. Or to say it another way, the church is not something you do, or just go to; the church is something you *are*.

Why does this matter? It matters because as we think about how to revive our joy in Christ, one of the primary ways we will do that is by intentionally meeting with God's people. Remember the warning issued by Bunyan about backsliding? He says they "shun the company of lively and warm Christians." It might feel uncomfortable to read this, but if you are drawing back from meeting with other believers, you are not helping yourself.

I understand why you might immediately object. It might be that church is really tough for all manner of reasons. Perhaps the needs of those in your Bible study group threaten to swamp you and you feel yourself pulling back to protect yourself from burnout. Perhaps instead you feel forever on the outside and struggle to connect at all, and even though you are with people you still feel lonely. Maybe it's interpersonal issues, discouragement over falling numbers or certain life circumstances, or a feeling of lifelessness causing you to want to stay in bed on Sunday mornings. When you do get yourself to church, you can easily name twenty things that could be done better—or twenty things you wish were done by someone else, but somehow it's always you on the rota and frankly, you're exhausted.

On the other hand, maybe there's nothing wrong with your church gatherings and you enjoy other Christians' company, but slowly you've got out of the habit and now there always seems to be something that comes up on a Sunday or on the night of the prayer meeting. Next week, you'll definitely make it a priority, but today you just need to get this thing done.

When it comes to issues in the local church, Paul had seen it all. Disagreements, disunity, and disgusting behavior. And yet he never tells Christians to back out of fellowship but rather, always to "encourage one another and build one another up" (1 Thess. 5:11). The author of Hebrews highlights exactly this point when he writes:

> "And let us consider how to stir up one another to love and good works, not neglecting to meet together, as is the habit of some, but encouraging one another, and all the more as you see the Day drawing near." (Heb. 10:24–25)

If you are stuck in your faith and are not gathering regularly with the church, you should not be surprised that you are feeling stuck. You have abandoned one of the great graces that God has given to his people to help them persevere and mature. Friend, resolve today to heed God's life-giving command to commit to your church fellowship and be with the ones that he has redeemed.

–

In Acts 2, the church is pictured as being together day-by-day in order to help support one another. Let me encourage you, then, to think of church as more than a weekly meeting on a Sunday but a group of people spurring one another on in the faith, so on that great day we stand before the throne together.

Meeting regularly with other Christians as you sit on their couches, eat food together, arrange play dates for kids, help with regular chores and home maintenance, *as well as* meeting together on a Sunday to worship (and, note in Acts, to celebrate communion together) will help you flourish in the Lord. Remember, God has not just come to save individuals but to save his church, your new brothers and sisters "which he obtained with his own blood" (Acts 20:28).

Believe It (Head)

In the New Testament, a significant metaphor used of the church is that it is Christ's body (Eph. 4; 1 Cor. 12). In those passages, there is a big emphasis on the fact that we are all members, or parts, of Christ's body and that we need all the other parts of the body for our own maturity and spiritual happiness. So, to put it starkly, you cannot say to Christ, "I love you, it's just your body I can't stand."

Is that how you view the church? Do you see the people of God as being there for your good?

Dietrich Bonhoeffer, the twentieth-century German theologian, captures this idea well when he writes:

> "... the Christian needs another Christian who speaks God's Word to him ... again and again when he becomes uncertain or discouraged ... The Christ in [a believer's] own heart is weaker than the Christ in the word of his brother; his own heart is uncertain, his brother's is sure."[5]

Bonhoeffer understands there are times in our relationship with Jesus when we do not see him for who he is and that is why Jesus gave us the church. It is exactly in those moments that we need to remind ourselves just how vital it is to see the faith of our brothers and sisters because doing so will show us just how glorious, and mighty, and gracious, and loving our King is.

To get very practical: Who in your church have you talked to about the fact you're feeling spiritually stuck? If the answer is no one, then make the decision right now to change that. God has given you fellow believers to spur you on. You need them right now. It might be hard to admit you are struggling. It might involve confessing sin or lowering the mask. It will involve being vulnerable, but you need fellow Christians to carry your burden with you right now and show you Jesus.

Love It (Heart)

I really want to emphasize that it is vitally important when we are stuck not just to navel-gaze, but to lift our focus away from ourselves and onto Christ and then others. The picture of the church as Christ's body shows us not only that we need others for our own vibrancy, but that *they* also need us. Yes, you read that right. Even when you are feeling in a rut, *you* can be a help to others.

One thing that will nurture our commitment to others and our devotion to the church is to understand just how precious other believers are to God, and therefore to us as well. Just think about this amazing fact: The church, with all its preposterous flaws and failings, is revealing the "manifold wisdom of God" (Eph. 3:10). The real church—not the ideal one, but the real one—that you are part of, and should be attending, is in union with Christ as a wife is with her husband (Eph. 5:22–23). Your congregation is part of the church universal—the people of God across time and around the world—who together will one day gather around the throne of God. The church is an outpost, a glimpse, of the coming global reign of God's Son.

So, as you gather with other Christians who have quirks, and loves, and fears, remember that they are members of Jesus' body as inseparable from him as your own fingers and toes are from you (1 Cor. 12:12–31). This is why Jesus, when he confronts Saul on the road to Damascus, doesn't say, "Why are you persecuting my followers?" but rather says, "Saul, Saul, why are you persecuting *me*?" (Acts 9:4, emphasis added).

Act on It (Hands)

Of course, not only do we want to believe and love the truths of this chapter; we also want to act on them. My prayer is that as you begin to move forward in the Christian life, you feel a sense of devotion and delight in your local fellowship of believers. In light of that desire, here are a few practical applications to help:

1. Be an active member in a healthy local church. This means being a member of a church that unapologetically believes the Bible is the Word of God without any mixture of error. It also means it'll be a place where the gospel is proclaimed weekly and where songs are sung that are filled with biblical content. It'll be a place that takes seriously the preaching of God's Word and meaningful membership. And it won't just be inward focused but intent on making disciples to the ends of the earth.

2. Make communion a priority. When we break bread together, we realign our hearts on Christ and his sacrifice. As we physically take, eat, and drink, we enact our total dependence on him. Just as we need food and drink to stay alive, we need Jesus to sustain us in this moment and forever. In the Lord's Supper, we proclaim, to ourselves and others, his death until he comes again (1 Cor. 11:26). This is a glorious reminder to us that one day we will enjoy a feast with our Lord.

3. Hang out regularly, and intentionally, with other Christians. Do not just gather with the church on Sundays (though please do this!) but spend time throughout the week with other Christians. Think of ways that you can incorporate seeing others into your schedule. Could you share the school run with another family? Could you run errands for an older Christian you know? Could you host or feed other believers who live nearby? When you meet informally like this, spur one another on,

> pray, and share encouragement, but also have fun, remembering that the Lord is gathering a people to himself for eternity.

As we think about how to persevere in our Christian lives, it is important to remember that we must become (or remain) devoted to a family that has God's glory and your good in mind. Together we will make it to glory, when we will see that running the race of faith was completely worth it.

Life in heaven will not be a kind of never-ending choir practice (that's not heaven; that's purgatory). In many ways, it will be much like it is here. You will spend eternity with these people you currently laugh and cry and walk and have coffee with, those you serve alongside on the kids' team and music group. We will sing together, but we will also eat together, work together, experience fun and recreation together, and—thankfully!—do it all without a hint of sin or the curse. All the sin that currently makes meeting together hard will be washed away forever and what we love about our spiritual family now will prove to be just a glimpse of the fellowship we will enjoy on that day.

5

The Mission

And the Lord added to their number
day by day those who were being saved.

Several years ago when I was in the midst of planting a church in North Carolina, several members kept telling me there was a book that I had to read. The book was called *The Hunger Games*. Of course, being a former college athlete, I waited for the movie to come out and watched that instead! But once I had, I found the storyline fascinating.

The movie (and book) is set in a dystopian future where an evil government hosts a gladiator-style, compete-to-the-death tournament for the country's twelve territories. The main character, a teenager called Katniss, befriends another girl called Rue from a different district. Sadly, during the course of the games, Rue is killed. In that moment, Katniss builds a burial site where she surrounds the body with flowers. She then deliberately turns to the camera, gives a three-fingered salute, touches her lips, and points to the camera. For those watching the Hunger Games from Rue's district, the gesture is seen as a sign of love and respect. Almost immediately, they erupt in rebellion against the government. What seems like a small thing—a simple hand gesture—sparks a movement powerful enough to eventually take down an evil regime.

The illustration is far from perfect, but it gives a sense of the type of advance that the gospel takes in the New Testament, from a tiny beginning to a world-changing force. It all starts in Acts 2 as Peter preaches at Pentecost and gathers the first church together where God adds to their number every day (Acts 2:41–47). From there, God's Kingdom advances as Christians are scattered and spread the gospel wherever they go. The newly formed churches then send missionaries out to rescue those who are perishing, make disciples, and plant more churches. Each gathering of believers becomes an outpost of the Kingdom of Light, waging war on Satan and pushing back spiritual darkness (Col. 1:13).

Each conversion sees sin and death lose a captive soul as it's reborn to spiritual life. Freedom replaces slavery and life replaces death as Jesus is preached and individuals turn to him.

The watching world is so shaken up by what happens in the early church that when Paul and his band of brothers make it to Thessalonica in northern Greece, the people say of them, "These men who have turned the world upside down have come here also" (Acts 17:6). And this disruption of evil and darkness hasn't stopped. The proclamation of Jesus' life, death, and resurrection continues to change whole societies and millions of people's eternities.

—

Why does this matter? Because I am convinced that one of the ways we get out of the rut of spiritual stagnation is by understanding that being part of the Christian faith means being part of something bigger than ourselves. When we feel stuck, we need to fight to expand our vision. It's a battle to do this, I know. Especially when we are struggling spiritually, life can seem like a monotonous drudge—shower, work, eat, sleep, repeat—or else our struggles can seem overwhelming and all-consuming. Either way we quickly lose our perspective and our purpose shrinks down to wanting to simply get through or escape or be comfortable.

But we—with all our failings and faults and at times mundane lives—are part of something world-changing. Collectively, we've been given a great mission (or Great Commission) to make disciples by evangelism (telling people about Jesus) and discipleship (growing together in the faith). The conversation we have today could, in God's grace, turn someone's life around. The meal we cook for an outreach event could play a part in someone's salvation. The love we show others in our church could intrigue our neighbor and be the beginning of them coming to faith. The encouraging message we send to a believer could spur them on to keep living for Jesus at work. The verse we share with a child could still impact them as an adult.

I think you get the point. As we look outside of ourselves to love others and serve the Lord, it bring us joy. It's a mission worth getting out of bed for. It gives us purpose and drive.

So, taking our eyes off ourselves, let's rejoice that we have a part to play in God's rescue mission, saving people from a lost eternity in hell and then spurring them forward as we press on to heaven together. Remember, this world will one day by renewed, and so will we! One day our weariness and struggle and tiredness and sin will be a distant memory, and instead, along with all the redeemed, we will enjoy life as it's supposed to be in the presence of Jesus forever. In heaven we will at last see the fruit of our service and know it was worth it.

There is no greater way—I would argue—to look beyond our own problems than refocus again on eternity and throw our energies into God's mission: helping bring people from the domain of darkness into the Kingdom of the Son and walking with them as they mature in Christ. There is nothing so encouraging as seeing lives changed by the gospel today.

Believe It (Head)

Right now, service—and especially evangelism—probably feels like the very last thing you want to do. I get that. My intention is not to guilt-trip you or add to your burden, but instead to gently challenge you to refocus on what you're living for. If it's anything less than to love God and to love others, it won't satisfy. And as we think about loving others, part of this will involve seeking to understand our role in sharing the gospel. The fact that believers are called by the Lord Jesus to go and make disciples is something that stands from generation to generation. Indeed, it was the Lord's last marching orders for his church.

As we think back on Acts 2, we can see that the work of evangelism and gospel proclamation is vital. Peter proclaimed the gospel and 3,000 were saved. Later we read the Lord "added to their number day by day those who were being saved" as the church loved one another and the apostles taught of Christ (Acts 2:47). How do we know this is what happened? Because Paul makes it clear in his letter to the Romans that people will not be saved without hearing the gospel (Rom. 10:9–17).

It seems to me that the early church was committed to simply sharing with others that they had met a loving Savior who, by his cross and resurrection, forgives and offers the hope of eternal life. Throughout Acts and church history, the kingdom goes forward as ordinary Christians share the good news that Christ has come and offered his life as a ransom for many (Mark 10:45).

Love It (Heart)

My parents have fifteen grandchildren and they cannot help but talk about them. Why? Because they treasure them. Let me ask the question: Would those who know you—or look at your social media posts—know that you love and treasure the Lord Jesus by what you talk about? Again, I'm not trying to guilt-trip but to diagnose a problem. When we are spiritually stagnating, we can easily stop cherishing Christ, and so we stop wanting to talk about him, either to Christians or non-Christians.

As we battle with our hearts to see and cherish Jesus, let's remember that part of this process involves sharing his goodness with others. When we do, we remind ourselves of his goodness even in the moment of telling someone else.

As we seek to speak of Christ, let's pray that he would stir our love for God and love for those we are trying to reach. After all, evangelism is fueled by our love for God's glory seen supremely in the holy God saving wretched sinners. And it is found in our love for our neighbor as we hope that they will experience the same grace we have experienced in the love of the Savior.

The good news, though, is that the Lord's yoke is easy and burden light (Mt. 11:30). We simply need to commend Jesus and leave the results to God. We are faithful to speak; he is faithful to save.

Act on It (Hands)

Practically speaking here are some simple ways you can begin to look outside yourself and join in with the mission of God to save people:

- **Pray for opportunities to evangelize**

  Identify specific networks in your life that contain unbelievers that you can pray for on a regular basis. Who in your family, friends, neighborhood, school, or place of work needs to hear the gospel? Pray for them regularly by name and share their names with your closest Christian friends.

- **Serve unbelievers**

  Seek out ways that you can help care for and do good for unbelievers that you know. Are there ways you can do this with your church family together?

- **Invite family and friends to church**

  There is little as powerful as a church that loves the Bible, proclaims the gospel, sings rich songs of biblical truth, and has a vibrant community, so share it with the non-Christians you know. Bring unbelievers into a place where they will hear the gospel and see it lived out.

- **Learn to share the gospel clearly and succinctly**

  Remind yourself how you came to the point of putting your trust in the Lord and then practice telling that story. Learn how to share your testimony in one minute. Think about some go-to questions that you can ask people you meet about their lives, then think of some things that you can share, perhaps starting the sentence with, "I find that trusting in Jesus has made an impact on my life in this way …"

In Acts 2, Luke writes that because of the commitment of the early believers to simple things like the gospel, the Scriptures, prayer, one another, and mission, they began to gain favor with the outside world; ultimately, the Lord used them to add to their number. At other points they encountered hostility and persecution, but through the church, the gospel spread from Jerusalem, to Samaria, to the ends of the earth; ultimately, through the course of time, it spread to you.

As we recapture our joy in the one who bought us at a great price and as we glimpse his passionate heart for the lost that we see around us, my prayer is that it might be said of you, dear reader, that those "who have turned the world upside down have come here also!"

Conclusion: Eyes on Jesus

I opened the book by asking if you've ever been stuck. Well, I do not write as someone unaffected by the problem. It's true that our own struggles are unique to us, but struggling itself is certainly not unique. I have been there, too. In those moments what I needed most was someone to remind me of the truth and to remind me that I am loved.

I do not know what your current state of being stuck looks like. It may be that you are stuck because of besetting sin, or it may just be that you have lost joy and vibrancy in your love for Christ. It may be that the Christian life feels more like duty than delight. Or it may just be that the busyness of life has allowed the temporary to crowd out more eternal things. Wherever you find yourself, I hope that you might be encouraged from my own story of struggle and, more than that, the incomprehensible love of the Savior.

As I close, I want to take you to a passage of Scripture that helped me during a particularly hard season. It's the story of Jesus healing the leper in Mark 1. At the time, I felt like a spiritual leper, and so it deeply resonated with me. Here's how Mark describes the encounter:

> "And a leper came to him, imploring him, and kneeling said to him, 'If you will, you can make me clean.' Moved with pity, he stretched out his hand and touched him and said to him, 'I will; be clean.' And immediately the leprosy left him, and he was made clean." (Mark 1:40–42)

In order to fully appreciate the story and understand its meaning, it's important to understand the context. Leprosy was *the* disease that Jewish people feared most. It was a detestable skin disease that overtook the body with painful boils and lesions. It was described by some as a death by inches. Yet, it was more than that because having leprosy meant that you were ceremonially unclean, too, and you had to live quarantined outside of the city. Then, to top it off, if you were ever in the presence of others, you were made to cry out "Unclean!" so that you didn't infect them. The Jewish historian Josephus said that in Jesus' day those with leprosy were "in no way differing from a corpse."

That is exactly this man's predicament. And it's not just for days, or weeks, or months, but this is his life with all of the stigma and pain it carries. Yet, in Mark's account, this desperate man does the unthinkable. He comes up to Jesus and instead of crying out "Unclean!" he begs for Jesus to show him mercy.

What is Jesus' response? Jesus is moved with pity. Jesus is moved with compassion. Jesus, in his mercy, reaches out and touches the leper.

Jesus' actions would have appeared unthinkable to those who watched on. Every time someone touched a leper they, too, became unclean. And more than that, as readers who have witnessed Jesus' power, we know that Jesus didn't need to touch the man in order to heal him. But by touching him, Jesus makes the unclean clean. Not only did Jesus minister to the leper's physical despair, but he ministered to his emotional anguish as he likely hadn't felt the touch of another human in years.

I remember the moment during my hardest struggle that helped me the most. I was hurting. I was down. I felt shame and hopelessness. It was at that moment that I ran into my high school basketball coach. He was far from an affectionate man. Yet, on that day, I remember breaking down and falling toward him. He caught me, embraced me, and spoke words of life and truth into my ear. That's what I needed in that moment.

Again, I do not know what you are going through, but Jesus stands with you, his arms outstretched ready to receive you, renew you, and recommission you.

If sin is your struggle, let me encourage you to start right now, as you read this, knowing in your heart that what John writes is completely true: "If we confess our sins, he is faithful and just to forgive us our sins and to cleanse us from all unrighteousness" (1 John 1:9).

If weariness is your struggle, know that when you seek him, though the road may still be rough, he promises that "they who wait for the LORD shall renew their strength" (Is. 40:31).

If distraction is your struggle, remember your very "life is hidden with Christ in God"—he holds you fast. "When Christ who is your life appears, then you also will appear with him in glory" (Col. 3:3–4).

What is most important is not a white-knuckling, try-at-all-costs Christian faith but the knowledge that you have a Savior who loves you, forgives you, receives you when you fail, and has given you his Holy Spirit to help keep going. Remember, you have a Savior who never failed once. Ultimately, the only way we will become unstuck and flourish with joy is by taking our eyes off ourselves and putting them on the only one who has the power to bring us safely to heaven.

> "Therefore, since we are surrounded by so great a cloud of witnesses, let us also lay aside every weight, and sin which clings so closely, and let us run with endurance the race that is set before us, looking to Jesus, the founder and perfecter of our faith, who for the joy that was set before him endured the cross, despising the shame, and is seated at the right hand of the throne of God." (Heb. 12:1–2)

Notes

1. John Bunyan, *The Pilgrim's Progress* (Oxford University Press, 2003), p. 145.

2. Thomas Chalmers, "The Expulsive Power of a New Affection", Union Publishing, www.unionpublishing.org/resource/the-expulsive-power-of-a-new-affection

3. Martin Luther, *Luther's Works, Vol. 51* (Fortress Press, 1966), pp. 77–78.

4. J.I. Packer, *Knowing God* (Hodder and Stoughton, 1973), p. 186.

5. Dietrich Bonhoeffer, *Life Together* (Harper and Row, 1954), p. 23.

Acknowledgements

This book would not have been written without the initiative, help, support, and encouragement of the whole 10ofThose team, as well as my family and co-laborers. To my bride Kelsey Akin. And also to Jonathan Carswell, Jonathan Pountney, Sheri Newton, and Siwan Davies, thank you for all your gracious help and support.